As parish volunteers

toral ministry of visit

need for a resource t~~hat combines helpful gu~~

visitation and suggestions for devotions. This guide is a

marvelous response to that need."

Margot Hover, D.Min.

Duke University Medical Center

Author, *Caring for Yourself When Caring for Others*

"This is an important resource and superb training tool for all those involved in ministry to the sick. It will help ministers bring consolation and peace, acceptance and serenity to the affected members of their families and communities."

Bridget Mary Meehan

Author, *God Delights In You*

"This book offers excellent training for lay ministries (though this 'professional' chaplain learned a great deal from the book) that can be used in formal training sessions, for individual study, and for those who want to review and refine skills as they share their gifts with the sick. Information. Skills. Prayer and ritual resources. It is a manageable book that needs wide circulation.

Rev. Richard B. Gilbert, M.Div., FCOC, FAAGC

Director, Connections-Spiritual Links

JOSEPH M. CHAMPLIN
SUSAN CHAMPLIN TAYLOR

A Thoughtful Word, A Healing Touch

A Guide for Visiting the Sick

TWENTY-THIRD PUBLICATIONS
185 WILLOW STREET • PO BOX 180 • MYSTIC, CT 06355
TEL: 1-800-321-0411 • FAX: 1-800-572-0788
E-MAIL: ttpubs@aol.com • www.twentythirdpublications.com

Acknowledgments

Excerpts from the English translation of *Pastoral Care for the Sick: Rites of Anointing and Viaticum* © 1982, International Committee on English in the Liturgy, Inc. All rights reserved.

Scripture excerpts are from the New Revised Standard Version of the Bible, copyright ©1989, Division of Christian Education of the National Council of the Churches of Christ in the United States of America. All rights reserved.

Fifth printing 2003

Twenty-Third Publications
A Division of Bayard
185 Willow Street
P.O. Box 180
Mystic, CT 06355
(860) 536-2611
800-321-0411
www.twentythirdpublications.com

ISBN 0-89622-637-9
Printed in the U.S.A.

CONTENTS

INTRODUCTION

For nearly forty of my sixty-four years I have served as a Roman Catholic parish priest. That long period of service in the pastoral ministry naturally included countless visits to the sick, calls made to ailing people in their homes or at local hospitals.

Susan, a niece half my age, understandably has had far fewer experiences with visiting the sick. But as a reporter and editor for two national magazines, first *People* and then *Modern Maturity*, she has learned to listen carefully and write well about this subject. With that background, Susan has written part one of this booklet, "Ten Useful Tips for Visiting the Sick."

I am well aware of how important it is to offer *spiritual* comfort to those who are sick and suffering. That prompted me to prepare parts two through seven of our booklet. Those sections respond to this need by offering parish ministers and other visitors practical guidelines as well as actual texts that they can use. These include sample prayers and scripture verses together with ways for introducing prayer and the Bible to those who are ill.

My niece and I agree that most people feel rather uncomfortable when faced with the task of visiting someone who is sick. They ask themselves with a bit of apprehension: "What will I say? How should I act?"

May these pages of useful tips and helpful tools ease that anxiety. May they also make your own visits to the sick more satisfying and most of all more beneficial for the people you are visiting.

ONE

TEN USEFUL TIPS FOR VISITING THE SICK

It's a situation most people have been in at some point in their lives: visiting a seriously ill friend or relative. Many people avoid such encounters because they feel they "don't know what to say." What do you say to someone with a serious illness without sounding trite or hollow? How can you turn such a visit into a healing encounter? Here are ten suggestions to help make the visit a positive one—for both you and the sick person.

1. Be There.

Fear of saying the wrong thing often keeps friends or relatives from visiting. The first step is to realize that it is your presence, not your words, that means the most. Remember, there is no magic formula, there are no magic words. Just being present for that moment will go a long way toward helping the person heal, if not physically, then at least emotionally.

2. Know the Power of Touch.

Holding a person's hand or giving a comforting pat on the arm can mean a great deal to someone fighting fear and loneliness. Naturally, it depends on your closeness to the person and on his or her willingness to be touched, but a visitor who stays at arm's length from the patient may be unconsciously exacerbating the sense of separation that a seriously ill person already feels. A gentle touch tells the person you're willing to be *with* them.

3. Listen.

Come to the visit with an open agenda. Let the patient lead in telling you what his or her needs are. If he or she wants to recount favorite stories—even if you've heard them several times before—listening with enthusiasm can validate the person's sense of self-worth.

4. You Don't Need the "Right" Answer.

A person confronted with a life-threatening illness often asks, "Why me?" Many visitors feel they are supposed to have an answer, one that will make the patient "feel better." But the familiar clichés one uses to make sense of the tragedy ("It's part of God's plan." "Everything happens for a reason.") can sometimes do more harm than good. The ill person frequently isn't really looking for an answer but is expressing his or her confusion. So the best thing to do is to repeat the question in your own words, indicating that you understand the person's anxiety. "I see you're really troubled by this" is a more helpful response than "God is testing you."

5. Validate the Person's Emotions.

Too often, because of our own discomfort, we try to avoid the subject of illness or death and don't allow patients to discuss their feelings. If they say, "I know I'm not getting better," responding with "Don't talk that way" does not help them come to grips with the situation. Instead of suggesting that they keep their feelings to themselves, encourage them to express their fears or concerns; this way they know that you're willing to journey with them, and that you understand their thoughts and emotions.

6. Don't Be Afraid of Tears.

Again, saying to a person, "Don't cry," is more hurt-ful than it is helpful. Tears help heal, and bottling up one's emotions is unhealthy. You don't have to say anything; you can just hold the person's hand. And don't be afraid of your own tears. Let them flow.

7. Try to Be Compassionate.

We can be better prepared to handle a patient's emo-tions if we know something about what he or she is experiencing. Terminal patients in particular experi-ence a variety of moods and emotions, among them anger, depression, denial, false hope, peace, and acceptance. There is no one formula for how and when they will experience these, but they are all com-mon emotions among the seriously ill. Try to be open to wherever they are at any given time so that you can respond with understanding and compassion.

Keep in mind, too, that anger and frustration may sometimes be directed toward loved ones. Visitors need to realize that this is not personal, but part of the response to the illness. Also, not every sick person experiences peace and/or acceptance. However, your visits will go a long way toward help-ing the person reach this goal if you are able to offer compassion, love, and acceptance.

8. Monitor What You Say.

Even if patients are unconscious or seem unaware of what's going on around them, they may be able to hear what is said to them. Thus visitors should not only guard against saying negative things, but should continue to express words of love and encouragement.

9. Keep Your Visit Brief.

Seriously ill people tire easily but may feel obliged to put on a good face for visitors. Frequent brief visits are better than infrequent long ones. Find out the best time to visit, and plan your call accordingly.

10. Be Yourself.

If you have always been an optimistic, upbeat person and carry that tone naturally into the sickroom with you, fine. But trying to put on a show of cheerfulness when you don't feel it will immediately strike a false note the patient will detect. Don't put pressure on yourself by feeling you have to "accomplish" something during the visit. You're there just to provide support, which the patient will appreciate more than any platitudes or jokes you may offer. As one hospice director says, "Remember, anything is the right thing to say as long as you're sincere."

TWO

GUIDELINES FOR PRAYING WITH THE SICK

Your First Visit

- Beforehand, carefully read the "Ten Useful Tips for Visiting the Sick" on pages 2-5.

- Then with two of these booklets in hand (one for yourself and the other for the person you are visiting), actually make your visit (and keep it relatively brief, perhaps ten minutes at the most).

- During this visit, connect or reconnect your relationship with the sick person through an easy conversation that focuses on the sick person. Listen a lot; say very little about yourself.

- Ask: "Is there anything I can do for you?" Generally, the answer will be no.

- Inquire: "Would you mind if I say a short prayer or read a brief passage from the Bible with you?" Normally, the response will be positive. If it is not, just assure the person you will be praying for her or him later. If the response is positive, proceed as follows.

- Select one or two "Prayers for Healing" from this

booklet (pages 9-16), that you think are suitable for this particular situation. Also select in advance one or two "Readings from Scripture" (pages 17-24) that you consider appropriate.

- Ask the sick person if he or she would like to join you in the prayers and reading biblical passages. If the answer is positive, hand the person a copy of this booklet and read the predetermined texts with or for her or him. (If the answer is negative, simply read the texts for the individual.)

- Tell the ill person that you hope to be back for another visit in the near future.

- Leave a copy of this booklet with the one who is sick.

- As you say goodbye, touch the infirm person in some way depending on your relationship, even if it is but a light grasp of the hand.

Subsequent Visits
- Before your subsequent visits, you might read Part One of this booklet again to again fix deeply in your mind its practical points.

- Try to make frequent, but brief visits, at least until the sick person has achieved near recovery. The concentration required during conversations with visitors drains their precious energy and can leave them quite exhausted.

- Your beginning conversations at each succeeding visit will probably flow more easily and become deeper. However, the focus should continue to be on the sick person, with particular attention to the various phases of his or her illness.

- Prepare and read several prayers and biblical passages with or for the sick person as you did during the first visit. The person may have developed a fondness for certain prayers and passages in this booklet. If so, use those in place of, or perhaps in addition to, the ones you have selected beforehand.

- If other people are present, invite them to share in the reading of prayers and passages.

- The comfort that ordinarily develops over repeated visits may encourage some visitors to pray spontaneously for the person they are visiting. (See the sample "Spontaneous Prayer" on page 16.)

- That same comfortableness may suggest the effectiveness of lengthier and more tangible use of a healing touch, like holding the hand of the person or even laying your hands on the person's head.

- Repeat your offer to assist in any way possible and make an honest promise to return soon.

Visiting a Person Near Death
In many and perhaps most cases this situation may be the expected state reached after a gradual decline observed through your repeated visits.

In addition to the prayer and passage steps followed in earlier visits, reflect on the recommendations in this booklet for comforting the critically ill (pages 25-27).

THREE

PRAYERS
FOR HEALING

There are different types of healing. A physical cure of some ailment is the obvious kind. We usually pray for that first. But emotional and spiritual healings are important as well. Sick people need courage to bear the pain; they need hope to lift heavy clouds of discouragement; they need wisdom to understand why this is happening; they need faith to recognize God's presence supporting them throughout these difficult days and weeks.

As we have seen, praying for or with a sick person may feel awkward or uncomfortable in the beginning. Using some of the familiar prayer formulas that follow may make that kind of prayer easier for both you and the one you are visiting.

PRAYING WITH THE PSALMS

The Lord Is My Shepherd (Ps 23)

This is perhaps the most frequently quoted passage from the Bible. Our God is a shepherd who constantly watches over us—feeding and refreshing us, guiding and strengthening us.

Lord, you are my shepherd; I shall not want.
You make me lie down in green pastures;
You lead me beside still waters;
   you restore my soul.
You lead me in right paths for your name's sake.
Even though I walk through the darkest valley
   I fear no evil,
   for you are with me.
Your rod and your staff—
   they comfort me.
You prepare a table before me
   in the presence of my enemies;
You anoint my head with oil;
   my cup overflows.
Surely goodness and mercy shall follow me
   all the days of my life;
And I shall dwell in the house of the Lord
   my whole life long.

A Plea for Help, Guidance, and Forgiveness
(Ps 25:1, 4–11)

When ill, we generally feel weak and confused. But we may also recall with regret our mistakes, poor choices, and sins of the past. This psalm places on the lips of the sick person those needs for help, guidance, and forgiveness.

To you, O Lord, I lift up my soul.
Make me know your ways, O Lord,
   teach me your paths,
   lead me in your truth and teach me,
   for you are the God of my salvation,
   for you I wait all the day long.
Be mindful of your mercy, O Lord,
   and of your steadfast love.
Do not remember the sins
   of my youth or my transgressions;
according to your steadfast love,
   remember me for your goodness sake, O Lord.
Good and upright are you, Lord;
   thus you show sinners the way.
You lead the humble in what is right,
   You teach the humble your way.
All of your paths
   are love and faithfulness,
   for those who keep
   your covenant and your decrees.
For your name's sake, O Lord,
   pardon my guilt for it is great.

A Prayer During Worry and Sorrow (Ps 116:3–5)
*Serious illness prompts sober thoughts and reminds us of our
mortality. The possibility of dying, not at some distant future
time, but at a moment uncomfortably close to the present,
can stir up anxieties and bring on sadness. The brief words of
this psalm, repeated often, may help with those fears and
that sorrow.*

The snares of death encompassed me;
the snares of the nether world
   laid hold on me;
I suffered distress and anguish,
   then I called upon the name of the Lord,
   "O Lord, I pray, save my life!"

Gracious are you and righteous;
   yes, you are merciful.
You protect the simple,
   when I was brought low, you saved me.
Return, O my soul, to your rest,
   for the Lord has dealt bountifully with you.

PRAYING WITH THE CHURCH

The Roman Catholic ritual book, *Pastoral Care of the Sick*, includes many formal prayers for those who are ill. Some are connected with the sacrament for the anointing of the sick. Others are for ordinary visitation of those burdened with illness. Here are a few of the latter that may prove comforting to sick persons and helpful for those who are visiting them.

A Prayer for Patience

Father, your Son accepted our sufferings
    to teach us the virtue of patience
    in human illness.
Hear the prayers we offer for our sick
    brother/sister.
May all who suffer pain, illness, or disease
    realize that they have been chosen to be saints
    and know that they are joined to Christ
    in his suffering for the salvation of the world.
We ask this through Christ our Lord.
R. Amen.

A Prayer for Health

All-powerful and ever-living God,
    the lasting health of all who believe in you,
    hear us as we ask your loving help for the sick;
    restore their health, that they may again offer
    joyful thanks in your Church.
Grant this through Christ our Lord.
R. Amen.

A Prayer for Endurance

> All praise and glory is yours, Lord our God,
>   for you have called us to serve you in love.
> Bless N. so that he/she may bear this illness
>   in union with your Son's obedient suffering.
> Restore him/her to health
>   and lead him/her to glory.
> We ask this through Christ our Lord.
> **R.** Amen.

For an Elderly Person

> All praise and glory are yours, Lord our God,
>   for you have called us to serve you in love.
> Bless all who have grown old in your service
>   and give N. strength and courage
>   to continue to follow Jesus your Son.
> We ask this through Christ our Lord.
> **R.** Amen.

For a Child

God of love,
  ever caring,
  ever strong,
  stand by us in our time of need.
Watch over your child N. who is sick,
  look after him/her in every danger,
  and grant him/her your healing and peace.
We ask this in the name of Jesus the Lord.
R. Amen.

Before Surgery

God of compassion,
  our human weakness
  lays claim to your strength.
We pray that through the skills of surgeons
  and nurses,
  your healing gifts may be granted to N.
May your servant respond to your healing will
  and be reunited with us at your altar of praise.
Grant this through Christ our Lord.
R. Amen.

SPONTANEOUS PRAYER

If you are comfortable praying for the sick in your own words, take the ill person's hand or lay your hands upon his or her head as you pray spontaneously. This type of prayer has a sound biblical basis: Jesus prayed and healed in this fashion; he also urged his followers to lay their hands upon the sick and, through praying with faith, to cure them. Here is a sample of this kind of prayer:

O all-powerful God, your Son Jesus
   touched the sick and healed them.
Look upon our faith
   and through our prayers and our hands
   may healing come upon N.
May he/she feel your power right now.
May he/she soon be restored to health.
May the clouds of discouragement
   immediately pass from him/her.
Give him/her courage to bear
   these sufferings and troubles.
United with Christ on the cross
   and Mary at the foot of the cross,
   he/she is winning many blessings for others
   here and in the world to come.
Fill him/her with peace. Amen.

FOUR

READINGS FROM SCRIPTURE

Passages from the Bible possess their own unique power for bringing comfort, understanding, and strength to those who are ill. The following could be read to, with, or by the sick person you are visiting.

A Promise of Refreshment (Mt 11:28–30)
"Come to me,
   all you that are weary
   and are carrying heavy burdens,
   and I will give you rest.
Take my yoke upon you,
   and learn from me;
   for I am gentle and humble in heart,
   and you will find rest for your souls.
For my yoke is easy,
   and my burden is light."

Jesus the Healer (Lk 7:18–22)

The disciples of John
   reported all these things to him.
So John summoned two of his disciples
   and sent them to the Lord to ask,
   "Are you the one who is to come,
   or are we to wait for another?"
When the men came to him, they said,
   "John the Baptist has sent us to you to ask,
   'Are you the one who is to come,
   or are we to wait for another?'"
Jesus had just then cured
   many people of diseases,
   plagues, and evil spirits,
   and had given sight
   to many who were blind.
And he answered them,
   "Go and tell John
   what you have seen and heard:
   the blind receive their sight,
   the lame walk,
   the lepers are cleansed,
   the deaf hear,
   the dead are raised,
   and the poor have good news
   brought to them."

A Believer's Power to Heal (Mk 16:15–18)

Jesus said to them, "Go into all the world
    and proclaim the good news
    to the whole creation.
The one who believes and is baptized
    will be saved;
but the one who does not believe
    will be condemned.
And these signs will accompany those
    who believe:
    by using my name
    they will cast out demons;
    they will speak new tongues;
    they will pick up snakes in their hands,
    and if they drink any deadly thing,
    it will not hurt them;
they will lay their hands on the sick,
    and the sick will recover."

Jesus Promises the Cross for His Followers
(Lk 9:23–26)

> Then he said to them all,
>> "If any want to become my followers,
>> let them deny themselves
>> and take up their cross daily and follow me.
> For those who want to save their life will lose it,
>> and those who lose their life
>> for my sake will save it.
>
> What does it profit them
>> if they gain the whole world,
>> but lose or forfeit themselves?
> Those who are ashamed of me
>> and of my words,
>> of them the Son of Man will be ashamed
>> when he comes in his glory
>> and the glory of the Father
>> and of the holy angels."

Jesus Calms the Storm and Our Fears
(Mt 14:22–33)

> Immediately he made the disciples
> > get into the boat
> > and go on ahead to the other side,
> > while he dismissed the crowds.
> And after he had dismissed the crowds,
> > he went up the mountain to pray.
> When evening came, he was there alone,
> > but by this time the boat,
> > battered by the waves,
> > was far from the land,
> > for the wind was against it.
> And early in the morning
> > he came toward them on the sea.
> But when the disciples
> > saw him walking on the sea,
> > they were terrified, saying "It is a ghost!"
> > And they cried out in fear.
> But immediately Jesus spoke and said,
> > "Take heart, it is I; do not be afraid."
> Peter answered him,
> > "Lord, if it is you,
> > let me to come to you on the water."
> He said, "Come," so Peter got out of the boat,
> > and started walking on the water, toward Jesus.
> But when he noticed the strong wind
> > he cried out, "Lord, save me!"
> Jesus immediately reached out his hand

and caught him, saying to him,
    "You of little faith, why did you doubt?"
When they got into the boat, the wind ceased.
Those in the boat worshiped him, saying
    "Truly, you are the Son of God."

Jesus on the Cross and His Mother by the Cross
(Jn 19:25–27)

Meanwhile, standing near the cross of Jesus
were his mother and his mother's sister,
Mary the wife of Clopas,
and Mary Magdalene.
When Jesus saw his mother
and the disciple whom he loved
standing beside her,
he said to his mother,
"Woman, here is your son."
Then he said to the disciple,
"Here is your mother."
And from that hour
the disciple took her into his home.

A Comforting Promise (Jn 14:1–3)

"Do not let your hearts be troubled.
Believe in God, believe also in me.
In my Father's house
there are many dwelling places.
If it were not so, would I have told you
that I go to prepare a place for you?
And if I go and prepare a place for you,
I will come back again
and will take you to myself,
so that where I am, there you may be also."

Note: If you are a eucharistic minister bringing communion to the sick person, you may want to include this reading.

The Bread of Everlasting Life (Jn 6:53–58)

So Jesus said to them, "Very truly, I tell you,
   unless you eat the flesh of the Son of Man
   and drink his blood,
   you have no life in you.
Those who eat my flesh
   and drink my blood have eternal life,
   and I will raise them up on the last day;
   for my flesh is true food
   and my blood is true drink.
Those who eat my flesh and drink my blood
   abide in me and I in them.
Just as the living Father sent me
   and I live because of the Father,
   so whoever eats me will live because of me.
This is the bread that came down from heaven,
   not like that which your ancestors ate,
   and they died.
But the one who eats this bread
   will live forever."

PARSE

FIVE

COMFORTING THOSE WHO ARE CRITICALLY ILL

The final struggle in our journey of life is a test of faith. Is there a life to come? Will I see God? How can I possibly cross the chasm between my finite human weakness or limitations and the infinite, divine majesty or holiness of God?

In addition, there is an enormous need for strength to bear intense physical pain, to overcome the deep discouragement caused by a lengthy illness, or to endure the sadness of leaving behind those we love.

When people are very seriously ill or near death, brief biblical texts can be of great support for them. The following phrases are best recited in a slow, quiet voice, alternated with periods of silence. Since the sense of hearing often remains operative after the other faculties seem to have lost their power, the words might be spoken softly into the dying person's ear, with each phrase repeated two or three times before moving on to the next one.

The darkness is passing away,
and the true light is already shining (1 Jn 2:8).

Who can separate us from the love of Christ?
(Rom 8:35).

Whether we live or die we are the Lord's
(Rom 14:8).

Love bears all things, believes all things,
hopes all things, endures all things
(1 Cor 13:7).

We have an everlasting home in heaven
(2 Cor 5:1).

We shall be with the Lord forever (1 Thes 4:17).

We know that we have passed from death to life
because we love one another (1 Jn 3:14).

To you, Lord, I lift up my soul (Ps 25:1).

The Lord is my light and my salvation (Ps 27:1).

Beloved, let us love one another, because love is
from God; everyone who loves is born of God
and knows God (1 Jn 4:7).

Because of our faith, we have peace with God
  through our Lord Jesus Christ (Rom 5:11).

My soul thirsts for the living God (Ps 42:2).

Though I walk in the shadow of death,
  I will fear no evil for you are with me
  (Ps 23:4).

Grace to you and peace from God our Father
  and the Lord Jesus Christ (2 Cor 1:2).

Truly I say to you:
  Today you will be with me in paradise,
  says the Lord Jesus (Lk 23:43).

In my Father's home
  there are many dwelling places,
  says the Lord Jesus (Jn 14:2).

God, who is rich in mercy
  and who loves us with a great love,
  gives us new life together with Christ
  (Eph 2:4–5).

May the God of peace make you completely
  holy and may your spirit and soul
  and body be kept sound (1 Thes 5:23).

SIX

WHEN SACRAMENTS ARE NEEDED

When a family member or someone you care about is in the hospital or will be confined at home for an extended period, inform your parish. That will alert the appropriate staff members and enable them to arrange for the community's prayers on the sick person's behalf. Moreover, they can offer the ill individual an opportunity for the sacraments of penance (reconciliation, confession), holy communion, and, when appropriate, the anointing of the sick.

If a person is seriously ill, summon a priest as soon as possible. The priest, in addition to offering an opportunity for penance, will minister the sacrament of the anointing of the sick, which includes communion and a variety of comforting prayers.

To be seriously ill does not mean that the sick person is only moments away from death. It does mean, though, that the illness must be more than a heavy head cold. In the church's words, to receive this sacrament one's health should be seriously impaired by sickness or old age. If there is any doubt about this, call the local priest and let him decide.

These official rites have several purposes and effects: to enable the sick person to bear the illness bravely and to fight against it; to restore the person to health, if it is to the individual's ultimate good; to strengthen the person during temptations; to deepen the individual's faith in God; and to relieve the person's anxiety over death.

Countless experiences have shown how these rites always calm and strengthen seriously sick people. Often they even bring a marvelous restoration to health.

PRAYERS BEFORE THE ANOINTING

Lord God, you have said to us
    through your apostle James:
    "Are there people sick among you?
Let them send for the priests of the Church,
    and let the priests pray over them
    anointing them with oil in the name of the Lord.
The prayer of faith will save the sick persons,
    and the Lord will raise them up.
If they have committed any sins,
    their sins will be forgiven them."

Lord, we have gathered here in your name,
    and we ask you to be among us,
    to watch over our brother/sister N.
We ask this with confidence,
    for you live and reign for ever and ever.
    R. Amen.

PRAYERS AFTER THE ANOINTING

General Prayers

Father in heaven,
  through this holy anointing
  grant N. comfort in his/her suffering.
When he/she is afraid, give him/her courage,
  when afflicted, give him/her patience,
  when dejected, afford him/her hope,
  and when alone, assure him/her of the support
  of your holy people.
We ask this through Christ our Lord.
R. Amen.

Lord Jesus Christ, our Redeemer,
  by the grace of your Holy Spirit
  cure the weakness of your servant N.
Heal his/her sickness and forgive his/her sins;
expel all afflictions of mind and body;
mercifully restore him/her to full health,
  and enable him/her to resume his/her
  former duties,
for you are Lord for ever and ever.
R. Amen.

For a Child

God our Father,
　we have anointed your child N.
　with the oil of healing and peace.
Caress him/her,
　shelter him/her,
　and keep him/her in your tender care.
We ask this in the name of Jesus the Lord.
R. Amen.

For an Older Person

God of mercy,
　look kindly on your servant
　who has grown weak under the burden of
　years.
In this holy anointing
　he/she asks for healing in body and soul.
Fill him/her with the strength
　of your Holy Spirit.
Keep him/her firm in faith
　and serene in hope,
　so that he/she may give us all
　an example of patience
　and joyfully witness to the power of your love.
We ask this through Christ our Lord.
R. Amen.

SEVEN

FINAL REFLECTION

Those of you who have read through or, better, used this booklet while visiting the sick understand now that our response to the questions, "What will I say?" or "How do I act?" is simple to describe, but not necessarily easy to do.

Just being present and listening with love guarantees successful visits to ill persons. They will always prove comforting to the visited and satisfying to the visitor.

However, to go beyond these steps, as you may have now experienced, by reciting pertinent prayers, reading biblical passages, and repeating inspirational phrases, enhances those visits.

The Lord says to such visitors: "Well done, good and faithful servants...I was sick and you visited me. Enter into the joy of the kingdom."

OF RELATED INTEREST...

Praying with the Sick
Prayers, Services, Rituals
Sandra DeGidio, OSM

A valuable handbook and resource for anyone who ministers to the sick. Offers practical suggestions with an empathetic approach.
0-89622-893-2, 64 pp, $6.95 (B-88)

Suffering Loss, Seeking Healing
Prayers for Pain-Filled Times
Evan Drake Howard

These prayers give guidance and comfort through the various stages of grief and help the aggrieved integrate different kinds of loss in a healthy and positive way.
0-89622-699-9, 48 pp, $4.95 (M-80)

How to Love Again
Moving from Grief to Growth
John Monbourquette

Combines psychology and spirituality in a unique manner to offer comfort in times of despair and describes the healing process that comes after loss.
1-58595-165-X, 176 pp, $12.95 (X-07)

I'm Still Dancing
Praying through Good Days and Bad
Rose Tillemans

These passionate, whimsical, and upbeat prayers express faith in the God of quiet gifts and of refreshment, of laughter and of justice, of refuge and of joy.
1-58595-237-0, 80pp, $9.95 (X-82)

TWENTY-THIRD PUBLICATIONS
185 WILLOW STREET • PO BOX 180 • MYSTIC, CT 06355
TEL: 1-800-321-0411 • FAX: 1-800-572-0788
Bayard E-MAIL: ttpubs@aol.com • www.twentythirdpublications.com